Sleepover Party!

Games and Giggles for a Fun Night

For my daughters Devan and Bailey: *You make every night a sleepover party*.

For my nieces, Ali, Julia, and Kate: *Many happy pajama parties*.

And my super friend, Mealie: *I miss the pillow talk*.

STERLING and the distinctive Sterling logo are registered trademarks of Sterling Publishing Co., Inc

Photos by Thomas Hopkins
Designed by Laura Case

Library of Congress Cataloging-in-Publication Data

McGillian, Jamie Kyle.
  Sleepover party! : Games and giggles for a fun night / Jamie Kyle McGillian.
      p. cm.
  Includes index.
  ISBN-13: 978-1-4027-2978-2
  ISBN-10: 1-4027-2978-2
  1. Sleepovers—Juvenile literature. 2. Children's parties—Juvenile literature. I. Title.

GV1205.M33 2007
793.2'1—dc22

2006029509

10   9   8   7   6   5   4   3   2

Published by Sterling Publishing Co., Inc.
387 Park Avenue South, New York, NY 10016
© 2007 by Jamie Kyle McGillian
Distributed in Canada by Sterling Publishing
C/o Canadian Manda Group, 165 Dufferin Street
Toronto, Ontario, Canada M6K 3H6
Distributed in the United Kingdom by GMC Distribution Services
Castle Place, 166 High Street, Lewes, East Sussex, England BN7 1XU
Distributed in Australia by Capricorn Link (Australia) Pty. Ltd.
P.O. Box 704, Windsor, NSW 2756, Australia

Printed in China
All rights reserved

Sterling ISBN-13: 978-1-4027-2978-2
        ISBN-10: 1-4027-2978-2

For information about custom editions, special sales, premium and corporate purchases, please contact Sterling Special Sales Department at 800-805-5489 or specialsales@sterlingpub.com.

Sleepover Party!

Games and Giggles for a Fun Night

Jamie Kyle
McGillian

STERLING

New York / London

www.sterlingpublishing.com/kids

Contents

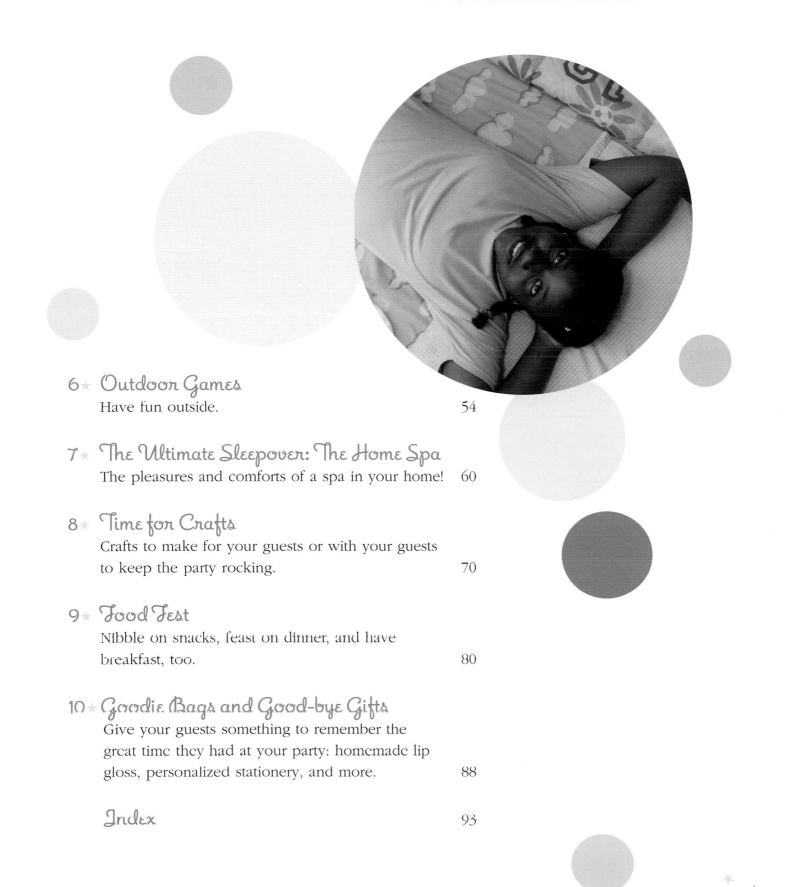

Introduction
It's Your Party!

What's more fun than a party with all your friends? A *sleepover* party with all your friends! Invite the gang over to chat, giggle, play, sing, munch, and dance the night away. In the morning, you may be a little short on sleep, but it'll be worth it.

A sleepover is a lot more than just the chance to show off your cute pajamas and see how long you can go without shut-eye. It's a way to turn new friends into close friends.

So kick back and have fun. Let off steam with a mega pillow fight. Tell your party pals about your latest crush and see what they think. Do some palm reading. Get your nails done. Send shivers down each other's spine with a scary story. Learn how to do something you've never done before. Or just act silly. It's all up to you, because it's *your* party!

This book is filled with ideas to make your sleepover creative, memorable, and lots of fun. So, c'mon, let's start planning!

Party Planner, That's You!
Sleepovers Are the Building Blocks of Friendships

"Lindsay had a tropical beach party sleepover. It was awesome. All the guests wore sunglasses and bathing suits and had colored zinc oxide on their noses. We painted a giant beach scene and hung it on the wall. Then we played games with beach balls. We drank frozen juice drinks and ate sandwiches on a beach blanket. In the morning, my face hurt from smiling too much!"

—Ali, 10, on her first sleepover

Sleepovers, slumber parties, pajama parties—what do you call them?

"I call them stay-up-overs!" —*Jackie, 10*

Sleepovers aren't just for birthdays—anytime is the right time to party!

Get a Clear Vision

First off, what kind of party would you like to have? Will there be a theme? Do you want to play loud music? Do you and your friends want to dance and sing? Will you and your friends dress up? Or, can you see them chilling at your dinner table in their shorts and T-shirts? Will dinner be served? What kind of food do you want to have? Can you imagine doing craft projects or baking? What about a guest entertainer? Would a family member or friend be willing to teach your friends Irish step-dancing, sign language, or knitting?

What's Your Dream Party?

Think about the kind of party you would like to host. Be creative. Give it a name. Describe the activities you might want to do at the party. Remember, there are hundreds of ideas from which to choose.

Figure Out If It Will Work

Now that you've decided what kind of party you would like to have, you need to decide if it's doable. Is your home large enough to accommodate your guests? If you had your sights on a round of basketball or Frisbee, is your backyard big enough? Do you have a playroom or den that you can use as your party room? Do you have your parents' permission to hang decorations, move furniture, and sleep in the party room?

"First, we ate pizza. Then we danced and had a blast with karaoke. Then Sierra made everyone laugh with her stories. I didn't know she was so funny. All that laughing made us hungry again. We baked yummy cookies, talked about boys, and made friendship bracelets. I never felt homesick. I had the best time."

—*Yvonna, 9, on her first sleepover*

Share It with the Troops

Get your parents' input to make sure your party plans can be carried out. And run your ideas by your friends—they'll probably have some great ideas too!

Set the Plan in Motion

Go back to your initial checklist and update it. Have your plans changed much?

Start with the basics: make invitations, buy party favors, create decorations, and think of adding special touches, such as stringing colored lightbulbs.

House Rules

They said yes! Once your parents give you the green light to host a sleepover party, make sure they know that you are up for the challenge. Let them know that you are willing to do the work that goes into throwing a party.

The Top 10 Things to Get Straight Before the Party

1. Look at the family calendar to settle on a date that works for everyone.
2. Decide with a parent how many guests will be invited. If this is your first sleepover, go for a smaller group.
3. Set up a specific time for the party to begin and end.
4. Decide with a parent if your party should include just snacks or dinner and breakfast the next morning.
5. Discuss with your parents if any part of the party will include boys. Make sure you stick to what you agree to.
6. Talk about where the guests will sleep. Will it be in your room or in another part of the house?
7. Review the menu. Be sure to shop for all the food you

need for dinner, snacks, and breakfast.

8. Discuss which rooms of the house are off-limits to guests.
9. Agree, in advance, on a time when lights are out.
10. Establish a code for your parents to let them know you need a little help managing the party.

Make Three Separate Lists

Two to Three Weeks Before the Party

★ Discuss party plans with a parent.
★ Make a guest list.
★ Make invitations and send them out.
★ Plan the menu.
★ Plan the theme and decorations.

One Week Before the Party

★ Buy the paper plates and decorations.
★ Write a shopping list for food and drinks.
★ Plan the goodie bags.
★ Arrange the music selections.
★ Make sure all guests have responded.

Day Before or Day of the Party

★ Clean the house.
★ Get out your sleeping bag.
★ Shop for the food and drinks.
★ Hang party decorations.
★ Blow up balloons.
★ Make party platters.
★ Pick out an outfit and a pair of cool pj's.
★ Make the goodie bags.
★ Run through the games and activities in your head.

Remember: Mom and Dad will be much more likely to let you host another sleepover if you help clean up after this one!

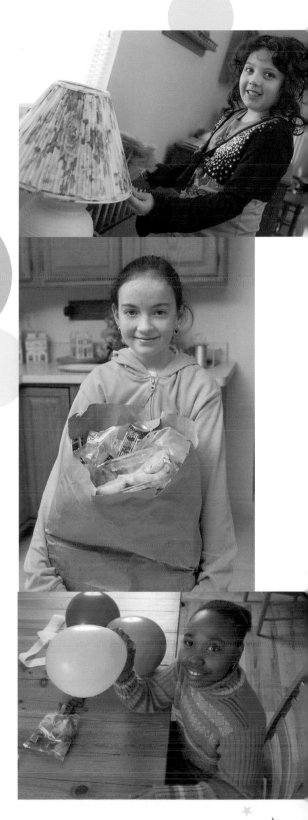

It's OK to Ask for Help!

No party planner can do it alone. Enlist the help of your friends. If you have an artsy friend, ask her if she can help with invitations and decorations. If you have a friend who's really into music, ask her what songs or musical pieces she would play or want to listen to. She may even be willing to share her CDs.

If you have a friend who loves to shop, ask her if she'd help you get some of the stuff you need.

Other partygoers may be willing to help:

* clean up before the party
* clean up after the party
* serve the refreshments
* set up the furniture in the party room
* give out game prizes
* decorate the room

Find a Personal Trademark

Put your signature on the party with something special to make your pals say, "Wow!" How about making handmade T-shirts with the date and the party theme written on them? (Fabric pens work great!) Or, if you like pink, how about you do all your details in pink? Pink outfits, pink pajamas, pink nail polish, pink headbands, and pink hair clips (the hair clips can be party favors)? If you're not really into pink, choose another color. Or, pick a pattern—how about jungle or floral prints?

What Makes a Perfect Finishing Touch?

Start thinking about simple touches that will create a party atmosphere, such as banners, balloons, flowers, candles, fabric throws, a pile of soft pillows, colored lights, and a boom box. Show your plans to your parents for their input.

What Makes a Cool Centerpiece?

How about a basket filled with party favors or a large framed photo of you and your friends?

If it's a birthday party, make the table bright, festive, and sweet by throwing confetti and streamers all over the table. And then, toss assorted wrapped candies all over your place settings.

Make a unique and easy floral arrangement. (See "Floral Fantasy in a Jiffy" in chapter 8.)

Invitations

Keep your invitations simple, but fun. Do them on your computer or make them by hand. You might want to design the invitation to look like a pillow or a pair of pajamas.

Custom Postcards

Another option is to decorate plain postcards with an assortment of stickers or rubber stamps. Make a pretty border on the cards with a felt-tip pen. Punch a hole at the top of the card. Tie a small piece of ribbon through the hole, or glue a piece of fabric, such as lace, onto the paper. Your friends will be saying, "Are you sure you didn't buy these?"

What's most important, when making your invitations, is to be sure to include all the party details: the date, address, time, and if there's something you'd like your guests to bring. Of course, you also want them to know that you're the one inviting them.

Don't Forget to Include R.S.V.P.

R.S.V.P. means "Let me know if you can come to my party so that I'll know how many party favors I'll need to get, how many hot dogs my dad will need to put on the grill, and how many place cards I'll need to write." When guests call to let you know if they can come, keep a guest list by the phone and check off each partygoer's name. Use this also as an opportunity to ask your guest if she owns a sleeping bag, if she has any food allergies, and if she can help in some way, such as by bringing a few CDs or an extra sleeping bag for someone who doesn't own one.

Menus

Plan food that is easy to prepare and fun to eat. (Check out chapter 9 for easy recipes.) But if cooking is not your thing, or Mom and Dad don't want you guys around the kitchen, invite each guest to bring a dish. That's called pot luck. But coordinate in advance so that you don't end up with five different kinds of potato salad!

Music

So, you want the best dance party ever, huh? Here's what to do. Gather your favorite CDs and place them next to your CD player before the party starts so that you won't forget them. You can put on the invitation that guests can bring two favorite CDs with them. (Tell your friends to write their names on their CD cases, so that when the party is over, you can return the CDs to their rightful owners.) By asking each girl to

---

R.S.V.P. is a polite way of reminding people of something that they should already know: If you receive an invitation, you should reply, even if you can't go to the party. R.S.V.P. stands for *"Répondez, s'il vous plaît,"* which means in French "Please reply." Nowadays, many invitations include a "regrets only" on the R.S.V.P. line. That means that as the host, you will count on seeing the guest at the party, unless she calls to tell you otherwise.

Why do we use the initials of a French phrase in an invitation that's written in English? That's because the French have strong ideas about manners. These ideas come from the French court of King Louis XIV, from the late 17th and early 18th centuries.

bring her favorite music picks, every girl will be moving and grooving, guaranteed!

Help Your Guests Feel Welcome

Make everyone feel comfortable and special by spending a few minutes one-on-one with each guest.

Show your thoughtfulness. Have something for each guest. If you know your friend Susie drinks soymilk, have some on hand when it's time for milk and cookies. If Jessie can't eat nuts, make sure you have snacks that are nut-free.

Cherish the Memories

Hang a large piece of poster board in the party room. As guests arrive, ask them to sign and decorate the poster board.

Keep a disposable camera on hand. During the party, you and your friends can capture all the fun by clicking away. After you develop or download the photos, you can make a sleepover scrapbook.

2 Theme Party

An awesome party often has an awesome theme. You get to choose one that suits you and your guests. Let your imagination soar!

Let's say you want to have a party with a sports theme. Make the invitation resemble a ticket to a sports event. Wear sweat suits. Serve hot dogs and other foods that you may find at a concession stand. Watch sports events on TV. Play sports trivia games. Have a championship tournament. Give out trophies. You get the idea!

Party Profile Quiz

Can't make up your mind about the perfect theme for your party? Take this Party Profile Quiz to find a theme that fits you and your best buds. Circle the response that best fits who you are.

1. Your idea of total fun would be you and your pals...

a. playing basketball or hockey, throwing a Frisbee, or skateboarding

b. hiking and camping and telling tales under the stars

c. reading and talking about your favorite books

d. listening to music, playing an instrument, and sharing opinions about your favorite music artists

e. going to the mall and window shopping for the absolute latest fashions

f. dancing, singing, and playing charades

2. You are best known for your love of...

a. sports

b. nature and animals

c. books

d. music

e. fashion

f. performing

3. Your style is...

a. Total Sportster—tracksuit, sneakers, ponytail

b. All Natural—jeans, sweatshirt, comfy shoes

c. Classic—khakis, sweater, barrettes, and headbands

d. Rock 'n' Roller—faded jeans, boots, T-shirt, leather jacket

e. Model Gal—designer jeans, miniskirt, trendy accessories, high-heeled boots

f. Stage Presence—clothes that look like costumes; a unique mixture of plain and fancy separates

4. It's important for you to...

a. play sports

b. be around nature

c. read books

d. listen to music

e. dress like a model

f. express yourself through song and movement

Your Score

- ★ If you answered two or more questions with a, host Sports Night.
- ★ If you answered two or more questions with b, host Under the Stars.
- ★ If you answered two or more questions with c, have a Bookworm Bash.
- ★ If you answered two or more questions with d, have a Music Party.
- ★ If you answered two or more questions with ε, host a Glam Girl Party.
- ★ If you answered two or more questions with f, have a Stage Night Soiree.

Sports Night

Celebrate your active life and your love of sports.

Invitation Idea

Make your invitation resemble a piece of sporting equipment.

Wear

Workout clothes, team uniforms, or sweats.

Eat

Have foods that you might find at a sports event, like hot dogs, popcorn, and soft pretzels. Drink sports drinks and water from water bottles. Serve fresh fruit and energy bars.

Play

- ★ Shoot hoops, hold relay races, ride bikes, play jump rope, throw Frisbees.
- ★ Play sports trivia, read sports magazines, watch sports events, talk sports, talk about which event you would want to participate in at the next Olympics.

Give

Cool sneaker laces, personalized water bottles, energy bars, sweat bands.

Under the Stars

You are outdoorsy, so why not hold the party in your backyard under the stars? If possible, set up a tent and sleep outside. If the weather doesn't cooperate, bring the tent inside. Put glow-in-the-dark stars on the ceiling and hang plants.

Invitation Idea

Draw the moon and the stars on the invitations. Ask guests to bring flashlights.

Wear

Hiking and camping gear with neon-colored wristlets and colored bandanas.

Eat

Have a barbeque. Make and eat s'mores (check out the recipe in chapter 9). Drink milk and eat freshly baked cookies in the shapes of moons and stars.

Play

★ Have every guest bring a flashlight. When it's dark, play tag. Players can use their flashlights to shine some light on the game.

★ See how long your guests can stay quiet to listen to the sounds of nature. Talk about what you hear.

★ Have each guest wish upon a star.

★ Share hiking adventures.

★ Gather around the pretend campfire for a sing-along.

★ Tell ghost stories.

Give

Photos of the campers, plastic canteens, colored rocks and stones, bags of homemade trail mix.

Bookworm Bash

Celebrate your love of books with a book party. Talk about the stories that you have read, and which characters you loved best.

Invitation Idea

Make the invitation look like a book. Draw a book worm on the cover. Write the info inside the folded invitation on the "open pages" of the book.

Wear

Arrive dressed as your favorite book character, and have your friends try to guess who you are. Stay in character for as long as you can.

Eat

As you discuss character and plot, enjoy cups of hot chocolate or herbal tea. Crunch on chocolate-covered biscotti. Dine on foot-long "hero" sandwiches.

Play

- ✦ Play Charades using favorite book titles.
- ✦ Write a group story. Pass around a notepad, and have each person write a few sentences. Read the finished story aloud. Experiment with mysteries, how-to, and romance fiction.
- ✦ Create your own book or magazine.

Give

Books, colored pencils, journals, homemade bookmarks.

Music Party

Create a music club atmosphere.

Invitation Idea

Make a ticket to the VIP room of a music club. Include the words "Admit one." Put a number on each ticket for a prize drawing.

Wear

Arrive dressed as your favorite music star. Can anyone guess who you are?

Eat

Munch on bowls of pretzels and cheese-flavored goldfish. Dine on sandwiches or burgers. Drink frozen juice.

Play

- ✦ Play a variety of music.
- ✦ Try karaoke.
- ✦ Act out songs and have friends guess the titles.
- ✦ Have music magazines and homemade and real instruments on hand.
- ✦ Play musical chairs.

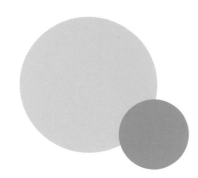

★ Play air drums and air guitars, and when the music stops, freeze.

Give

Recordings of your favorite songs.
Homemade drums and shakers.

Glam Girl Party

If fashion is your passion, enjoy this spoof.

Invitation Idea

Ask your guests to take part in an exclusive fashion event.

Wear

Glamorous outfits.

Eat

Your favorite fancy foods.

Play

★ Do beauty and hair makeovers.
★ Give manicures and pedicures.
★ Act like fashion models during a photo shoot.
★ Have a fashion show. Give each guest a turn at walking down the runway. Take photos of each guest in a fabulous outfit.

Give

Photos of each girl on the runway, sequin change purses, sparkling nail polish wrapped in small colored cellophane bags.

Stage Night Soiree

You and your friends love to perform, so turn your party into a stage event.

Invitation Idea

Make it resemble a program for a play. Include your guests' names as a cast of characters or a list of activities you've planned labeled Act I or Scene 2, as in a real play.

Wear

The sky's the limit. Dress as a pop diva, a movie star, a ballet dancer, or even a belly dancer.

Eat

Colorful, exotic foods. Ask guests to bring a favorite mystery dish.

Play

* Fill a trunk with dress-up stuff: wigs, hats, gloves, boas, shawls, and sunglasses. Use these items as props for guests to try on to create new characters.
* Give each guest 5 minutes of fame. Let them act, sing, dance, do impressions, or tell jokes. Videotape it, if possible.
* Make up a dance routine and perform it for an audience.
* Talk about favorite movies.
* Create a routine to perform at the next local talent show.

Give

Sunglasses or autograph books.

3

Great Guests

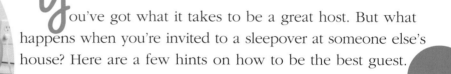

Y ou've got what it takes to be a great host. But what happens when you're invited to a sleepover at someone else's house? Here are a few hints on how to be the best guest.

What to Pack

Here's everything you'll need for your evening out.

★ special pillow (Better yet, make your own; see "Me Pillows," on page 71.)
★ sleeping bag (or thick blanket)
★ your favorite pj's
★ fuzzy slippers
★ bathrobe
★ hairbrush
★ hair accessories
★ toothbrush
★ toothpaste
★ hand towel
★ jeans and a T-shirt for the next day
★ disposable camera
★ magazines
★ small flashlight
★ bathing suit (for warm-weather parties)

How to Keep the Party Hopping

Best-Guest Secrets

Smile

A smile is like an open door. It says, "Hey, I don't bite. Talk to me. Let's share a laugh." If you smile, chances are, someone else will smile too. Go for a smile chain. That's a bunch of smiles in a row. If you have a roomful of smiles, you are bound to have an excellent time.

Be Up for Anything!

Maybe you didn't plan on playing board games, or you thought that you would be having pizza for dinner instead of peanut butter and jelly sandwiches. Or, maybe you expected some other friends to be at the party. Well, whatever it is, don't get all hot and bothered. Let it go. Take the lead from your hostess, and try to have the best time possible. Give the impression that you're easygoing and up for anything.

Share Your Feelings

What do you do if the conversation isn't flowing like a waterfall?

Talk about favorite songs, movies, books, and TV shows. Chat about funny things that have happened to you or members of your family.

What can you remember about a vacation? Did something unusual happen during a holiday break? Did you take a vacation to a special place?

After you tell your story, ask someone else to tell hers. Give everyone a chance to speak. Don't worry about pauses in your chats. Conversation is an art that takes practice. If all else fails, talk about your favorite celebrity crush.

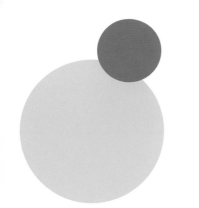

Wear What's Comfortable

A guest wants to look stylish and comfortable. But she shouldn't take attention away from the hostess. A few days before the party, ask the hostess what she plans to wear to the party. If she says, Capri pants and a pretty top, wear something comparable. If she says a frilly party dress, feel free to wear a dress, but without the frills. If your hostess is wearing jeans and a sweater, keep it casual.

Mind Your Manners

Be a model guest. Don't do anything you wouldn't do in your own home.

Do

* ⭐ Do clean up after yourself.
* ⭐ Do help with the dishes and clear away garbage.
* ⭐ Do be friendly and polite toward your friend's family members.
* ⭐ Do offer to help take photos, serve drinks, and set up games.

Don't

* ⭐ Don't leave your bags at the door.
* ⭐ Don't open your friend's kitchen cabinets or the fridge without permission.
* ⭐ Don't wander around the house.
* ⭐ Don't yell or make too much noise.

Sleepover Advice

Is your little brother just waiting to spoil your fun? Do you get butterflies in your tummy every time you think about sleeping at someone else's house? Whatever the problem, you can work it out.

I want to have a sleepover, but...

"I really want to have a sleepover, but the problem is Jimmy, my little brother. He is only four, but he is a huge pest. Jimmy acts up whenever I have friends over. He takes my stuff, makes embarrassing comments, and even hits me. I end up getting mad and yelling at him. How will I ever host a sleepover?"

—Bettina, 9

Hey, Bettina,

Little brothers are sometimes hard to deal with, aren't they? Maybe your parents can talk to Jimmy. If he has a reward for good behavior set up with Mom or Dad, say a shiny new toy or a trip to the park, he might behave better. Or, maybe Jimmy can have a play date planned for some of the time during your party. That will give you a nice breather. And when Jimmy does come home, you can let him meet your friends and share a snack before he goes to bed. That shouldn't be too painful!

★ ★ ★

"I went to a sleepover a few weeks ago. Everything was going along fine, but then a couple of the girls started to argue about what games they wanted to play. Things got out of control, and by the end of the party, three girls weren't talking to each other. I want to have my first sleepover, but I don't want anyone to fight."

—Mia, 10

Hi, Mia,

Here are a few ideas to keep things cool at your first sleepover. First of all, think small. Not more than three or four girls. Also, have a plan. Know the games you'd like to play. Have several craft ideas and materials set up. Before the party begins, ask each guest to be up for some new things. Explain that the party will be more fun that way. Keep in mind that some girls just might not want to play certain games. That's

OK, too. Have a bunch of cool books and magazines on hand. They can hang out while the rest of you play.

I want to go to a sleepover, but...

"I'm afraid that if I go to my friend's sleepover, I will get homesick. I don't know the girl too well, and I haven't met all her friends. She seems really nice though. I want to go, but I don't know if I can handle it. What should I do?"

—*Marnee, 8*

Hello, Marnee,

How about getting psyched to go, at least for part of the night? You can play games and get to know the girls, and if everything goes well, sleep over. Before the party, arrange to have a parent pick you up before lights out, say at 10 P.M., just in case you have doubts toward the end of the evening. You can always change your mind. If anyone asks, just say that you're tired and you need the comfort of your own bed. But let the girls know how much fun you've had.

★ ★ ★

"OK, here's my problem. I snore really loud. I just moved here, and I don't feel comfortable enough to let these girls know. I don't want to be teased. I'm invited to a birthday sleepover for a girl named Monica. I want to go, but the snoring thing is telling me I should just stay home. What do you think?"

—*Gracie, 12*

Howdy, Gracie,

A lot of people snore. It's not the worst thing in the world. Chances are, by the time everyone falls asleep, nobody will know you're a snorer because they will be out cold. Or, they might not hear you over their own snores. Remember this: We all make the occasional embarrassing sounds. That's just the way life goes. Concentrate on making friends and just having fun.

★ ★ ★

"I'm a health nut. I know I won't want to eat the food at the party. There's going to be pizza and cake, and I don't eat those things. I don't want to seem rude. Do you have any ideas for me?"

—*Talia, 13*

Hello, Talia,

That's cool. Don't feel bad about being someone who eats healthful food. Here's what you do. Eat a good dinner at your house before you go. Bring a large platter of fresh veggies with you, and ask the host if she wouldn't mind serving it so that you can have a snack. (Make it large enough, because I bet that some of the girls might want to have some too.) You can also bring a bag of fruit, cheese, or nuts to leave in your friend's kitchen. When the girls eat a snack that you would rather not have, munch on one of your own snacks. If you don't make an issue out of it, nobody else will.

4

Party Icebreakers

Great Games to Get Your Party Started

Your soccer pals don't know your school friends. Your school friends don't know your buds from acting class. And your buds from acting class don't even know you play soccer, let alone have friends from the team. How will you get all these good people together? Instead of putting your guests in a room to fend for themselves with small talk and bean dip, throw them into silly situations and let the games begin. Start the party with these games and challenges, and everyone will soon feel right at home.

Think Positive

Make everyone feel special.

Before the party

Have colored construction paper, felt-tip pens, and tape on hand. Write each guest's name at the top of a piece of paper.

At the party

Each girl gets a blank page taped to her back with her name written on the top. Then ask the girls to walk around the room and talk to each guest and write something positive

about each girl they've met on the paper. For instance, Chloe's paper might say: *very caring, animal lover, adventurous, loyal friend, kind, great laugh, pretty hair, happy girl.* When everyone has finished writing compliments about each girl, remove the tape from the paper and let each guest read her positive comments. These make nice keepsakes and can be taken home and posted on a bedroom wall.

Who Am I?

It's a case of missing identity! As guests try to find out who they are, laughter fills the room.

Before the party

Think of colorful characters from television, books, and movies. Write the names of these characters onto long strips of paper.

At the party

Tape a strip of paper onto the backs of your guests as they arrive. Explain that everyone has to figure out who is posted on her back by asking the guests (who can read everyone else's back but their own) questions such as "Am I a female character?" or "Am I a superhero?" or "Do I do anything funny?" Guests should respond as if the person is really the character. When a guest correctly guesses her own identity, reward her with a pair of sunglasses, a lollipop, or temporary tattoos.

Play Forgetful

Forgot something? Find out who will remember!

Before the party

Ask each guest to come to the party with something missing: one sock, lip gloss on only one side of the mouth, or wearing two different shoes, two different earrings, or two different shoelaces, for example. (You may want to write this on the invitation.) Have paper and pencils on hand for your guests.

At the party

Challenge your guests to put together a list of what each guest is missing. No peeking while writing! Whose list is the most complete?

Don't Change the Subject

This game is hilarious because players must keep talking. The results are sometimes outrageous.

Before the party

Fill a party hat with crumpled-up colored strips of paper that contain words for players to use as conversation starters. Try some of these: *Chinese food, amusement park, skeleton, string bean, potpourri, skateboard, blanket,* and *dinosaurs.*

At the party

Have one player at a time select a strip of paper from the hat, read it to herself, and immediately begin talking about the topic. The player must stay on the subject and keep making sense for 3 minutes, without stopping or pausing. Who will run out of things to say before changing the subject? Who will break down with a case of the giggles?

Who Are You Talking About?

Before the party

Write a fact about each guest. For example, you might write, "born in another country," "has more than two brothers," "plays guitar," and "speaks Chinese." Write all of the statements together on one piece of paper, and give each guest a copy.

At the party

As your guests mix, have them ask each other questions to determine whose name belongs with each statement. Whoever has the most names filled in after 5 minutes wins.

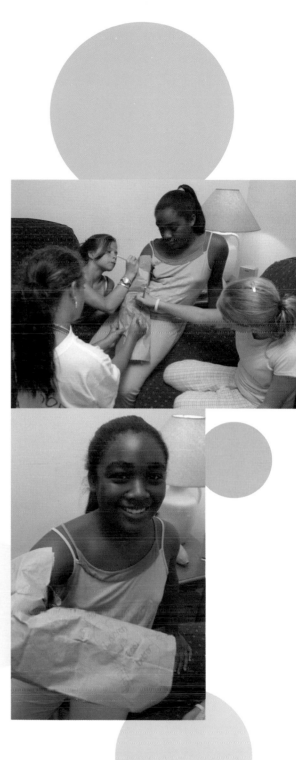

Sign My Arm

Now you don't need the cast to get the signatures!

Before the party

Have brown paper bags (lunch-size) for each guest. Also, have felt-tip pens for everyone.

At the party

Have everyone place a paper bag over the hand and forearm with which she writes. When the hostess gives the go-ahead, everyone in the room must get as many signatures as possible. It isn't so easy because each person has to keep the paper bag on her signing hand and sign with the opposite hand. After 3 minutes, the person with the most signatures wins! Try and find out whose names are on each player's paper-bag "cast."

Nickname

Can't afford to give your friend a gift? Give her a nickname. They're fun, especially when good friends give them to you!

Before the party

Have paper and pencils on hand. Also, have a hat.

At the party

Divide the guests into pairs. Give each pair some time for chit-chat. After a while, have the girls gather. Ask each girl to jot down a flattering nickname for the girl with whom she was paired based on her chat. Have each girl write the nickname and place it into a hat without anyone seeing it. After all the nicknames are in the hat, say each one out loud and have the rest of the girls match the nickname with the right girl.

Ask It Anything!

This is a great game to play while you're mixing and mingling.

You and your friends write a list of questions that require "yes" or "no" answers. Here are some suggestions.

★ *Am I going to get straight A's?*
★ *Will I be a cheerleader?*
★ *Do I have what it takes to be a rocket scientist?*
★ *Will I travel the world?*
★ *Will I be rich?*
★ *Will I get married?*
★ *Will I have kids?*

Use the picture below as your playing board, or draw it onto a larger piece of poster board before the party. You'll also need a coin.

To play

Give each girl a turn. Players ask the question aloud and then toss the coin over the game board. The coin lands on the response that answers your most pressing questions.

Count on it!

Try again. I'm not getting anything.

Probably not, but don't sweat it.

Better ask someone you trust for advice.

The answer lies in your heart.

There's a 50-50 chance that it will happen.

Not happening in this century.

Yes, most definitely!

5

Indoor Games

Choose any of these games—they're all fun. The first two are simple games that have been around for ages.

Pickup Sticks

This game is also known as Jackstraws. You don't need much to play—just a pile of drinking straws.

Before the party

Have a pile of colored straws. (You can substitute sticks or toothpicks.)

At the party

Hold a bundle of straws about 6 inches (15 cm) off the ground and then drop them. The first player tries to remove just one straw at a time from the pile without moving any of the surrounding straws. A player's turn ends when a straw wiggles as the result of taking away another straw. When the next player goes, she gathers up the straws and drops them again to create a new pattern of straws. The player with the most straws wins.

Blind Girl's Bluff

This game for four or more people is usually played outside, but it can also be fun in a large room without much furniture.

Before the party

You'll need a blindfold.

At the party

One player is blindfolded and stands in the center of the room. As the other players dart around her, she must try to tag them. When the blindfolded player catches another player, she then tries to guess who it is. For clues, she can try to touch the player's face and hair. When the blindfolded player guesses the identity of the tagged player, that person puts on the blindfold and the game continues.

Eyes, Nose, Mouth

You have to be quick with this game.

At the party

Players form a straight line with a leader facing them. The leader says, "Eyes, nose, mouth." When the leader says "eyes," the players touch their eyes. When she says "nose," players

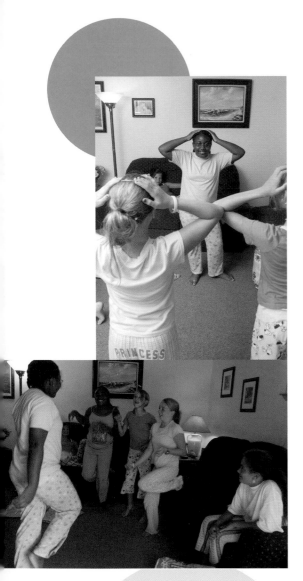

then touch the nose. But when she says "mouth," players must do what the leader does and not what she says. If the leader touches another body part, such as her left arm, when saying "mouth," the players should also touch the left arm. A player who touches her mouth, instead of doing what the leader demonstrates, is out of the game.

Susie Says

Here's a female version of the game Simon Says.

At the party

The leader faces the players and makes simple commands such as "Susie says, place your hands on your hips," or "Susie says, shake your hands in the air." Players must follow the commands. But when the leader says, "Bring your hands down by your sides," the players must ignore the command because the leader did not say, "Susie says."

Do I Know You?

This is a good game to play if your guests are all friends.

Before the party

Have paper and pens on hand.

At the party

Divide the girls into pairs. Ask each pair of buds any or all the questions from the list below. Have each girl write her answers on a separate sheet of paper. Then find out who knows her friend the best by having some game-show fun.

Pick someone to be the show's host, and ask each girl to guess her friend's responses. Winning pairs can celebrate their friendship by making friendship bracelets for each other.

★ *What color is your friend's room?*
★ *Is she a dog lover or a cat lover?*

* *What does your friend want to be when she grows up?*
* *Does she prefer chocolate or vanilla?*
* *What's your friend's best sport?*
* *What toppings does your friend like on her pizza?*
* *What's her favorite book?*
* *What's your friend's favorite season?*
* *If your friend had a dream vacation, what would it be?*
* *What does your friend like on her hamburger?*
* *What was the biggest laugh you shared?*
* *Who's your friend's celebrity crush?*
* *If marooned on a desert island, what five things would your friend hope she had with her?*
* *Does your friend prefer red, pink, or purple nail polish?*
* *What's your friend's favorite candy bar?*
* *What's her favorite song?*

Work It, Girl!

This is good for larger parties.

Before the party

Make a list of machines, such as an elevator, toaster oven, waffle iron, hair dryer, computer, printer, washing machine, popcorn popper, and paper shredder. Write each one on a strip of paper, and throw the strips into a hat.

At the party

Divide the girls into teams of four. Explain that each team will pick a strip of paper out of a hat. The team will have 60 seconds to figure out a way to demonstrate what's written on the paper without using any props. Once each group has gotten its imaginary machine up and running, the other teams have to guess what kind of machine the team is using.

Hold It

This game is similar to musical chairs.

Before the party

Stuff a plastic bag with everyday objects, such as a roll of toilet paper, a shoe, a ruler, a book, a paper plate, a rubber glove, a box of crayons, a shoebox, and a tennis ball. Have as many objects as you'll have guests.

At the party

Start by placing all the objects on the floor. Play your favorite music while guests walk in a circle around the objects. When the music stops, everyone must grab an item. Take away one object before starting the music again. A person who doesn't grab an object in time is out. The winner is the person who manages to get hold of the last object.

Tongue Twist

Challenge your friends to say a mouthful.

Before the party

Write tongue twisters on strips of paper. Crumple them up and place them in a hat. Try some of the ones below or make up your own.

She Drew It

How good are you at turning words into pictures?

Before the party

Have pads and felt-tip pens ready for each player.

At the party

Explain to your friends that this is similar to the game Telephone. Begin with a line of players, and give them all paper and felt-tip pens. Whisper a phrase to the first player, such as "Why did the chicken cross the road?" or "Girls rule, boys drool." Instead of that player whispering the phrase to the next player, she has to pass the message on as a drawing without talking or writing words. The next player looks at it, draws her interpretation of it on her sheet, and passes it to the next player. Once the message has passed to the end of the line, have each player write the phrase she tried to draw on the back of her paper. Compare the first drawing with the last. How many players got the original phrase correct?

Chop-Chop Relays

It's a race against time!

Before the party

You'll need two pairs of chopsticks, two brown paper lunch bags, two trays, and assorted buttons, hair combs, pencils, crayons, and spools of thread. Make sure you have as many items from each category as you have players.

At the party

Set up a course with a starting line and a finish line. In the middle area, arrange the buttons in one place, the hair combs in another, the crayons in another, and so forth. Divide the players into two teams. On the count of three, the first player from each team must pick up one of each object using the chopsticks. Give each player a tray to carry all the items to the finish line and drop them in the paper bag. Each team must collect items as quickly as possible—no time for slowpokes! The team who manages to get all their items in the paper bag first wins!

Under Your Spell

If you can spell it, you can play it!

Ever notice how some words are unusually difficult to spell and even harder to pronounce? Have a spelling bee with your friends. Here are some really excellent words with which to challenge your friends. Remember, it's just for fun!

* *plethora*
* *soothsayer*
* *conundrum*
* *pungent*
* *mediocre*
* *quell*
* *reincarnation*
* *cornucopia*

Balloon Bust Relay

Want a cool way to give out goodie bags? Put the loot inside the balloons and have relays with them. Play this game outside, but in case of rain a large room that doesn't contain breakables will do.

Before the party
Buy large balloons. Stuff them with tiny prizes such as stickers, whistles, and temporary tattoos. Then inflate the balloons and tie them. You will need one balloon for each guest.

At the party

Divide the guests into two teams, and place each team behind a starting line. Place the balloons at the other end of the room. A player from each team must run to the other end of the room, grab a balloon, and pop it. She can pop it any way she wants as long as she doesn't use a sharp object. When the balloon pops, the player collects the prize and then races back to her teammates. The game continues until everyone has retrieved a prize. The first team to pop all their balloons wins.

Musical Sleeping Bags

A good game to play after everyone has changed into pajamas.

Before the party

Arrange the sleeping bags any way you want. Have someone on hand to play music.

At the party

Have your friends parade around the room while the music plays. When it stops, each player must get in a sleeping bag in order to stay in the game. After each round, remove a sleeping bag. Keep playing until only one girl and one sleeping bag remain.

Hold Hands

Easy tasks become a handful!

Before the party

Have these materials on hand: a watch, a cord, a naked doll and doll clothes, a gift box, wrapping paper, tape, and a shoe.

At the party

Have players split up into pairs. Each pair stands hand-in-hand with their adjoining hands tied together with cord. With their free hands (one with the right hand and the other with the left one), the pairs must dress a doll, wrap a gift, and tie a shoelace. Which pair can complete these tasks in the least amount of time?

Pass the Hat

No hands, please!

Before the party

Have two hats available. Use party hats or cowboy hats.

At the party

Have your friends form two circles, one inside the other. One player in each circle wears a hat. The object is to pass the hat around the circle. The only catch is, the players can't use their hands to pass the hat from head to head. They can use their

feet, elbows, or necks. The team that passes the hat around the circle first wins.

Pass the Parcel

Everybody gets something. It's a win-win situation.

Before the party

Wrap a small gift, such as a keychain, lollipop, or candy necklace, into a layer of newspaper. Use a piece of tape to secure the object to the newspaper. Then wrap another layer of newspaper around that and tape another prize. Keep doing this until you have wrapped at least one gift for each guest.

At the party

Form a circle. Play music and pass the parcel around. Have someone volunteer to work the music. When the music stops, the player holding the parcel unwraps a layer of newspaper and gets the prize. Prize winners leave the circle so that each girl gets a present. You can also write fortunes, jokes, or messages on the newspaper to be shared with the crowd.

Get Dressed!

How long does it take you to put on your clothes?

Before the party

Fill two garbage bags with equal amounts of hats, scarves, mittens, shoes, belts, and other accessories, plus oversized sweatshirts.

At the party

Two players compete against the clock to be the first one to put on all the items in the bag. Make it even more of a challenge by timing each player. Create teams and have players call out, "Hurry, get dressed!"

Light as a Feather, Stiff as a Board

Did you invite the spirits?

At the party

Dim all the lights and tell your guests to be very quiet. One girl lies on the floor. Everyone else sits around her on their knees with index and middle fingers resting under the girl's body. One person is the storyteller who sits by the head and tells a creepy tale about the life and tragic death of the person lying on the floor. At the end of the story, everyone chants, "Light as a feather, stiff as a board," as they lift up the body a few inches (centimeters) off the ground with their hands. The idea is to have everyone believe that spirits are actually helping to lift the body off the ground. Take turns telling a story about each guest.

Can You Do It?

Calling all trivia buffs.

Before the party

On small strips of paper, write your favorite trivia questions, such as *"How many legs does a spider have?"* or *"Which planet is farthest from the sun?"* Blow up balloons and insert a strip of paper with a question inside each balloon. Place these balloons in Bag A. In Bag B, have a bunch of blown-up balloons with silly commands written on strips of paper inside them. Here are some examples.

- *Try to touch your nose with your tongue and lift your left leg in the air.*
- *Hold your arms up in the air for 3 minutes and recite a poem.*
- *Perform a dance routine and pretend you are a famous ballerina.*

At the party

When it's her turn, have each player reach into Bag A, pull out a balloon, and pop it. If the player can answer the question correctly, she stays in the game for another round. If a player cannot answer correctly, she must pull a balloon out of Bag B, pop it, and do what the paper inside says. If the player cannot carry out the command, she's out of the game. The game is over when all the questions have been answered. The person who answers the most questions correctly is the winner. Make a crown out of colored paper and write "Queen of Trivia" on it. The winner wears the crown for the night.

Musical Party Freeze

You can't go wrong with this game!

Before the party

Set up a dance floor and have a boom box on hand. Someone will need to start and stop the music. Someone will need to be the freeze police.

At the party

Begin by playing your favorite dance music. Players dance around the room. When the music stops, everyone must freeze. The freeze police watch for movement and take out players who are not frozen. Players who are out can either cheer for other players or keep dancing on another part of the dance floor. The winner is the one who's left.

Murderer

Don't look over your shoulder or you might be the next victim!

Before the party

Get a hat and strips of paper. Have a strip of paper for each guest. Leave all but one strip blank. Write "murderer" on that strip.

At the party

Explain to the group that each person picks a strip of paper out of the hat. The person who gets the strip that says "murderer" must select her victims without being detected. She blinks at her victims to signal them. When the victim realizes that she's just been "murdered," she counts to three and falls to the ground. Keep playing until everyone has had a turn to be either the murderer or the murdered. As everyone gets the hang of the game, your guests will become eager to stay alive!

Be a Star!

Have fun with this!

Before the party

Set aside a place for three judges to sit. You may want to make paper hats or nameplates for them. Also, clear an area for the contestants to perform.

At the party

Your guests are invited to audition to become the next American singing star. Have each contestant belt out a tune. Be as serious or as silly as you want. Let the judges ask the contestants questions about the songs they picked. Then the judges must decide who is going to Hollywood and who is staying home. If you can videotape these performances and watch them later before bedtime, it will be even more fun.

Palm Reading

If you spot a guest yawning or picking her teeth, it's time to show your friends your palm-reading talents. Your pals didn't know you could tell their fortunes, but now they will!

Palm reading, or palmistry, is the ancient art of reading the hands. A palmist may study the thumb, the lines on the palms, the shape of the fingernails, the fingerprint types, and all the markings in between the lines on the palm, to gain insight into a person's life and to see where her strengths and weaknesses lie. You may not be able to do all that, but you can read your friends' hands by following some basic palmistry principles.

Basic palmistry principles

Read the active hand. If someone is right-handed, read the right hand. If someone is left-handed, read the left hand. (The passive hand is used to read inherited characteristics.)

There are three main lines on the palm. The top line is the *heart line*, the middle line is the *head line*, and the bottom line is the *life line*. (Learn these lines by heart.)

Every hand is unique. No two are exactly alike. But the lines on your hands change. They stretch, disappear, widen, lengthen, and shift with time.

Now you can look at the three main lines on each guest's palm, and interpret what they might mean. Share what you find with them. Then your friends can compare their palm lines. What do they see about themselves? About each other?

Matters of the heart

The heart line is the top line. It is closest to the fingers.

If your heart line is high and far from the middle line, you have great passion. But you may also be a little on the jealous side. A lower heart line—that is, a line closer to the middle line—means you are a balanced person. A heart line that curves upward is a sign that you are outgoing and emotional. If your heart line is curved as it runs across your hand, you are romantic and poetic. The more sweeping and curved a heart line is, the more romantic and passionate you are. If your heart line is not one clear line, but resembles a line of chains, you are a big flirt.

Using your head

The head line is the middle line. It tells about your personality.

The stronger the head line is, the more forceful your personality tends to be. If the head line runs straight across, you are a focused person. A short head line that is strong means you can concentrate fairly deeply. You may be really good at projects that take a lot of patience, such as crafting and making jewelry. If you are imaginative, you will probably have a well-formed and slightly sloping head line.

Life on the Line

The bottom line (more vertical and curved), known as the life line, refers to how a person lives her life, not how long a person will live.

A longer line means that you get out there and live—you take advantage of all your opportunities. If your life line is a good distance from your thumb, you are generous with your time and energy.

Head-2-Pillow

Nobody will be bored with this board game.

Before the party

Create a board or path like the one shown below. Make playing pieces with each girl's name written on a piece of cardboard or construction paper cut into a cool shape. Use a coin to move about the board. Heads means move one space. Tails means moves two spaces. Or toss a single die (from dice).

Make up a rap song about your own hairstyle to perform for the girls.

LOSE A TURN.

Tell who your hero is.

Name three things you wouldn't want to be without on a deserted island.

Turn off the lights. Get a flashlight and create a puppet show using your fingers and shadows.

Share a secret about yourself.

MOVE BACK ONE SPACE.

Sing your favorite tune for the crowd.

Tell a joke, even if you have to make it up.

LOSE A TURN.

Perform a magic trick, even if you don't know magic.

Tell the plot of your favorite book.

MOVE AHEAD TWO SPACES.

Describe a dream outfit.

SKIP AHEAD A SPACE.

Sing the jingle from your favorite TV commercial.

MOVE BACK ONE SPACE.

What's your favorite sport? Can you invent a new sport?

If this were a masquerade party, what would you dress as?

Describe an awesome day in your future.

Tell what TV character you most resemble.

Describe yourself in four words.

Create a cool handshake for you and your friends.

Tell your pals a bedtime story.

If your pillow could talk, what would it say?

Say good-night.

PLACE HEAD HERE.

Finish Line

Outdoor Games

$\mathcal{S}$ome of these outdoor games involve getting wet. Make sure to tell guests in advance to bring their bathing suits if you plan to play.

Hunt in the Dark

There's nothing like a nighttime scavenger hunt.

Before the party

Hide some cool stuff out in the backyard, such as small rubber spiders, headbands, bracelets, key chains, temporary tattoos, whistles, barrettes, wrapped candy, and nail polish. You'll need a flashlight for each girl.

At the party

Give each girl a flashlight and a list of things to find. Let the search begin.

Narrow Necks

This is a warm-weather outdoor game because players will need lots of space to run and it's likely that water will be spilled.

Before the party

You will need two beach chairs, an area in which to run, two large plastic pitchers, two blindfolds, access to a hose, and two empty plastic 2-liter bottles with narrow necks.

At the party

Divide your pals into two teams. A person from each team sits on a beach chair, holding the empty plastic liter bottle between her knees as still as possible. A player from both teams is handed a pitcher filled with water. Both players get blindfolded and race to the seated player. Then the blindfolded player must pour the water from her pitcher into the plastic liter bottle. The team to finish the task and spill the least amount of water wins.

If you don't have pitchers handy, you can set up a tub of water and use large plastic cups or use 1-liter bottles for carrying water for your relay.

Spider

Work together to get to the finish line.

Before the party

Have colored chalk or tape and a whistle.

At the party

Make two circles and a starting line with the chalk or the tape. Divide the players into two teams. Have each team huddle together in a circle. Have everyone in each team link arms around each other to make a giant spider. When the whistle blows, both "spiders" must make their way to the finish line. Which spider will win?

Water-Balloon Volleyball

Prepare to get wet. Very, very wet!

Before the party

Set up lots of water balloons and store them in a bucket. Also, you'll need at least one beach towel for every two players. You'll also need a volleyball net.

At the party

Divide the guests into two groups. Pair them off and give each pair a beach towel. One side begins by placing a water balloon in the center of their towel. Each player holds the corners of the towel in her hands. The object is to toss the water balloon over the net using a towel and have the opposing side catch the balloon in their towel. The volley continues until one side misses and the balloon bursts, giving the other team a point. If you don't have a net, have two pairs volley back and forth from towel to towel.

Or, you could try tossing the water balloon without a towel.

Water Limbo

How low can you go?

Before the party

Set up the hose.

At the party

Make sure your guests are prepared to get wet. Have one person hold the hose, and have everyone else limbo under the stream of water. Lower the stream after everyone has had a turn going under it. If someone touches the stream of water, she's out. The last player to get wet is the winner.

Watch Out for the Snake

Did someone say snake?

Before the party

Set up the hose and have a blindfold on hand. Also, set up parameters for where the playing field should be.

At the party

Have everyone pretend that the hose is a snake. Blindfold one person who holds the hose and moves the stream of water all around. Everyone tries to dodge the water. The first player to get wet is the next blindfolded person who holds the hose.

Go Through Hoops

Watch out! Obstacles are everywhere!

Before the party

Arrange a course for your guests by setting a trail of outdoor-
Add challenges, such as a beanbag toss, a jump rope, and a
hula hoop.

At the party

Challenge your guests to go through tunnels and hoops.
Award the one who makes it through the course in the best
time with a silly prize, like a rubber duckie.

The Ultimate Sleepover: The Home Spa

Everyone loves to be pampered. Creating home spa treatments can make for an awesome sleepover. Here's how it works.

Set the tone by playing relaxing classical or New Age music. Serve juice drinks and veggie platters. You and your friends can chill out while sampling these beauty treatments. Of course, we know that your hair, nails, and skin look beautiful just the way they are; this home spa is just for fun.

You'll need a large room with enough chairs for each girl. Also, you'll need access to a sink, and a work space for mixing and mashing the ingredients. If you're doing manicures and pedicures, you'll need a work space for that, too.

You may want to create three separate stations: one for the hands and feet, another for the face, and the third for hair.

10 Steps to a Great Spa Party

1. Take *Before* photos of you and your guests before their beauty treatments begin.

2. Ask each girl to bring a large plastic bag containing a plastic tub for soaking her feet, a foot brush, a hand towel, and a face towel.

3. Try to enlist helpers beforehand, such as your mom, older sister, or family friends, to mix the beauty treatments. Also, have a few helpers on hand to take on mess patrol. Keep paper towels handy in case of spills.

4. Don't rush through each spa treatment. Relax—you have all night.

5. Be practical. You can't completely change your party room into a spa, but you can make a few changes that will make a difference. For example, hang a banner with your spa's name, play relaxing music, and put out piles of magazines, colored stones, and pretty candles. (Don't bother lighting the candles.)

6. Give everyone a chance to be pampered. Also, give everyone a chance to be a helper.

7. Make sure you protect all work surfaces and have supervision when it comes to mixing the ingredients and separating the egg white from the yoke.

8. Make sure everyone agrees to help clean up before the guests go to bed.

9. Flip-flops make a perfect party favor for this theme. Friends can wear them as toes are drying after pedicures.

10. Take *After* shots and use them to make a scrapbook and to give as good-bye gifts the next morning.

Hands On!

Here's a simple way to give a manicure.

★ Soak hands, one at a time, in a small bowl with warm water and scented soap.

★ Dry each hand. Remove any old nail polish with a cotton ball and nail polish remover.

★ Trim nails with a nail clipper.

★ File nails with an emery board.

★ For a special treat, massage each hand with scented cream. Rub the palm area and lightly tug on each finger.

★ Apply clear or colored nail polish and a protective top coat.

★ Let dry.

★ If you wish, apply decals.

Caution

It's best if you don't share items such as combs, nail files, nail clippers, and even nail polish. Sometimes you can pass an infection or even nail fungus to someone else or even from nail to nail. Of course, it's OK to share prepared face masks and other pampering lotions and potions.

Soaking nails too long can make the nails loosen from the bed and invite fungus. This is rarely a problem, however, until you're much older.

Also, do NOT ever get a hair dryer near water, and do NOT use a hair dryer when soaking feet or hands. Make sure your hands are dry whenever touching a hair dryer. This spa party does not entail using a hair dryer.

Hands and Feet Station

Feet Up!

Every foot loves a pedicure. Before the polishing stage, soak those tired feet in something sweet-smelling. Use a brush to rub off the flaky skin. Apply moisturizing lotion, and massage it into the feet and calves. This will feel very relaxing! Remember to ask each girl to bring a plastic foot tub and a towel, but you still might want to have extras on hand.

Here are some potions to tickle those tootsies.

Happy Feet!

For each pair of feet, you'll need:

- ★ 1 cup (240 ml) lemon juice
- ★ 5 shakes of cinnamon
- ★ 2 Tablespoons (30 ml) olive oil
- ★ ¼ cup (60 ml) milk

Mix it up and pour it into the foot bowl. Soak feet for 10 minutes. Dry the feet; don't forget to dry between the toes.

The lemon and cinnamon will smell heavenly, and the milk and oil will condition the skin.

Strawberry Feet Forever

Fruity delight for the feet

For each pair of feet, you'll need:

- ★ 1 Tablespoon (15 ml) kosher salt
- ★ 5 large mashed strawberries
- ★ 2 Tablespoons (30 ml) olive oil

Mix it all up and rub the mixture onto the feet. Use a foot brush to scrub away dead skin. Rinse with cool water. The coarse salt will help rub off dry skin.

Your pals will love the strawberry scent.

Face Station

Face It!

Here are seven steps to prepare the face for the fun.

1. Wash it.
2. Pat it.
3. Mask it.
4. Rinse it.
5. Tone it.
6. Refresh it.
7. Moisturize it.

Remember to ask your friends to bring their own face and hand towels. But you might want to have a pile of clean washcloths on hand, just in case…

Be sure to keep all face masks, toners, and lotions away from the eyes and mouth.

Exfoliate

Exfoliators help remove dry or dead skin cells. Along with other ingredients, they can be made with (dry) rolled oats and kosher salt. If you want to gently scrape away dead skin, try this mask.

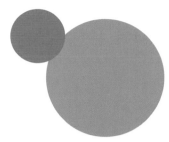

Oats 'n' Honey Mask

Per face:

- ★ 2 Tablespoons (30 ml) rolled oats
- ★ 2 Tablespoons (30 ml) plain yogurt
- ★ 2 teaspoons (10 ml) honey

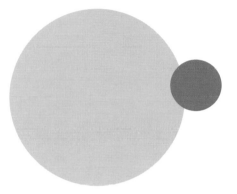

Mix it up and put it on the face. Rub lightly with fingertips in circular motions. Rinse with warm water.

Tone

Astringents help tone the skin. They remove excess oil and create a balanced skin tone. Along with other ingredients, they can be made with lemon juice or grapefruit juice. To get that just-right skin, try the two astringents below.

Lemon-up Mask

Per face:

- ★ 1 egg white
- ★ juice of ½ lemon

Whisk the egg and the lemon juice together. Apply to the face. Leave on for 15 minutes. Rinse with warm water.

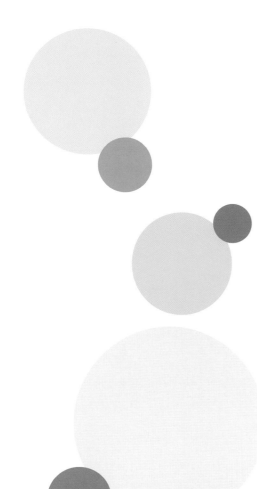

Grapefruit Delight

Per face:

* 1 egg white
* 2 Tablespoons (30 ml) grapefruit juice

Mix it up and put it on the face for 10 minutes. Rinse with warm water. The skin will glow!

Soothe

Soothers refresh and revitalize tired skin. Try this remedy of sliced cucumbers to relieve puffiness under the eyes.

Cucumber Comfort

Per face:

* 2 slices cucumber

Cover each eye with a cold slice of cucumber. Lean back and relax. Think about green things. Think about cold things. Now it's probably time to discard your used cucumber slices.

Steam

A steam treatment relaxes and soothes your face, but be careful not to burn yourself. Have an adult supervise this one!

Steam Tea Tent

Per face:

- ★ 2 cups (480 ml) water
- ★ 2 to 3 herbal tea bags (Chamomile is good.)
- ★ washcloth

Bring the water to a boil. Carefully pour the water into a large heat-resistant bowl. Add tea bags. Wait a few minutes so that it's not scalding-hot. Then cover your head with the towel and breathe in the steam from the bowl. Enjoy for about 5 minutes until your skin feels dewy. Then rinse.

Moisturize

Moisturizers make skin smooth, supple, and silky. Mineral oil, beeswax, cocoa butter, avocado, and banana replenish the oils in the skin. Try the banana misture or the milk-and-honey mask below.

Happy Banana

This nondrying banana mixture will make you happy.

Per face:

- ★ ½ banana
- ★ 1 Tablespoon (15 ml) honey
- ★ 2 Tablespoons (30 ml) sour cream

Mix it up and coat the face with it. Keep it on for 15 minutes. Gently wipe it off with a wet washcloth.

67

Milk-and-Honey Mask

This mask freshens dull and dry skin and feels wonderful.

Per face:

* ★ 1 egg white
* ★ 1 Tablespoon (15 ml) of honey
* ★ 3 Tablespoons (45 ml) powdered milk
* ★ 1 teaspoon (5 ml) liquid glycerin (from a drugstore)

Mix it all up. Put it on the face with a brush or fingers. Use all of the mixture. Relax for 15 minutes. Rinse with warm water.

Lotions and Potions

Also, have a variety of store-bought face creams and lotions on hand. Let the girls try on their favorites. You may want to ask your friends to bring moisturizers from home to share.

Don't rub lotion anywhere near the eyes. Of course, you don't want to get it in your nose or mouth either. Yuck!

Hair Station

Head Case

Before styling, condition your hair with one of these two mixtures.

Mayo Halo

Take ½ cup (120 ml) of mayonnaise and 1 Tablespoon (15 ml) of lemon juice and massage it into the scalp. Wrap hair in foil or plastic for 10 minutes. Rinse well. Run a few

Tablespoons of lemon juice through the hair as you are rinsing to make the hair smell good. This is ideal for normal hair.

Honey Banana

Mash a ripe banana in a small bowl. Add 1 teaspoon (5 ml) of honey. Massage into wet hair and leave in for 10 minutes. Rinse well with warm water or seltzer for added shine.

8 Time for Crafts

$\mathcal{F}$eel like getting crafty? Try some of these projects. Most are easy, but check the Project Difficulty Meter before tackling them. (The Project Difficulty Meter is explained on the opposite page.) You may want to ask your guests to bring supplies or materials with them to the party. Otherwise, the crafts can get expensive. You can include what they need to bring on the invitation so that guests will have time to prepare. Many supplies can be found in arts and crafts stores or in fabric stores.

Where to Find Supplies

When was the last time you checked out your local crafts store? If it has been a while, or if you've never been inside a crafts store, it's definitely time to go. Ask Mom or Dad to take you and help you plan for your party. You can find neat kits to make anything from key chains and handprints to jewelry boxes, stuffed animals, masks, and much more. You'll get tons of ideas just walking up and down the aisles. You can make great hats, awesome personalized shopping bags, and adorable shell creatures, to name just a few fun projects. It's well worth the trip.

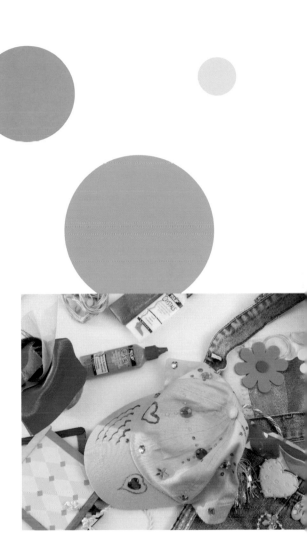

Also, check out fabric stores; they have some great stuff, too. Ask the sales assistant for fabric scraps when just a little will do.

Me Pillows

Project Difficulty Meter = 3

You can make these Me Pillows as gifts for your guests before the party, or you can create them together. Consider asking guests to bring along some neat fabric scraps, such as faux fur. The coolest pillows are the ones with real personality. Make a face out of scraps of materials. Frame the face with yarn for the hair. Write your name on the pillow, along with words that describe you. Guests will like having a small pillow to take home.

You'll Need

- ★ pillow cases or pre-made pillows (Find pillows in a crafts store or re-use old throw pillows.)
- ★ pillow stuffing
- ★ fabric scraps, ribbons, and bows
- ★ scissors
- ★ buttons, beads, or sequins (optional)
- ★ fringe, faux fur, or decorative borders
- ★ fabric glue
- ★ lavender spray or fruity cologne

Cover the work surface with newspaper.

If you start out with a pre-made pillow, simply decorate it with a variety of materials. Use colorful fabrics to spell out the letters of your name. Glue the letters to the surface. Add a fringe or a neat border.

If you are using a pillow case to make a pillow, fill it with stuffing. Seal the open end with fabric glue. Let it dry for about an hour before you begin decorating. Draw pictures of objects, like a guitar, soccer ball, or bike, that are special to you. Create a pattern with stripes or fringe.

You can always decorate the pillow with fabric shapes, buttons, beads, or feathers. Just keep in mind that if you plan on resting your head on the pillow, you'll want to keep the surface soft and smooth. Spray the finished pillows with scented spray, if you wish.

Floral Fantasy in a Jiffy

Project Difficulty Meter = 1

Make this as a centerpiece for your party, or ask your guests to bring these materials so that everyone can create a floral fantasy to take home. Ask the guests to bring an empty coffee can and a package of colored straws. You can provide the rubber bands, ribbons, and flowers.

You'll Need

- ★ 1 large empty coffee can per guest
- ★ 1 package of colored plastic straws for each coffee can
- ★ 2 wide, long rubber bands per can
- ★ wide, brightly colored spool of ribbon
- ★ fresh, dried, or plastic flowers

Wrap two rubber bands around the center of the coffee can. Line the outside of the can with a row of straws, and secure them by placing them under the rubber bands. Hide the rubber bands by tying a pretty ribbon around them. Fill the vase with your favorite flowers.

Hang-Wraps

Project Difficulty Meter = 2

Decorate the party room with these colorful squares or diamonds.

You'll Need

* small squares of wrapping paper, old magazines, or old photos
* craft sticks (or Popsicle sticks), four for each guest
* felt-tip pens
* white glue
* colorful yarn
* scissors

Cover the work surface with newspaper.

Cut a small square of festive wrapping paper about the size of a small photo.

Color four craft sticks.

Tie a long piece of colored yarn around one craft stick. Attach the string to either the middle of the stick so that the Hang-Wrap will hang as a square or in the corner so that it will hang down as a diamond.

Glue one stick along each side of the square to create a frame along the front border of your wrapping paper square.

Tie the yarn so that it hangs from a doorknob, or tack it to the ceiling.

Alternate: Spice up this craft by replacing the wrapping paper with a magazine picture of your favorite celebrity or with an old photo of your friends. Frame it with the craft sticks. Hang these colorful squares anywhere around the room. Guests will love to take these decorations home with them.

Silly Sleepy Eye Masks

Project Difficulty Meter = 2

Make masks that capture your personality and block the light!

You'll Need

- ★ cardboard cutout of an eye mask
- ★ scissors
- ★ felt pieces in glow-in-the-dark neon or pastel shades or patterns
- ★ felt-tip pens
- ★ colorful yarns
- ★ hole punch
- ★ fabric glue
- ★ elastic

Cover the work surface with newspaper.

Let each guest use the cardboard cutout to trace the shape of the eye masks onto felt or fabric. Cut the masks out of material with scissors, using the lines as a guide. Have the girls decorate their eye masks with relaxing bedtime sayings, such as *Sleep Tight* or *Sweet Dreams*. Guests can draw thick eyelashes onto the masks, or they can decorate them with eyeballs or *Z*'s.

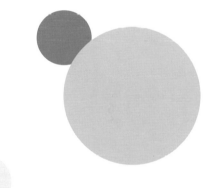

Create holes on both sides of the mask using a hole punch. Secure a piece of elastic through the hole on one side of the mask, and holding the mask up to cover your eyes, measure the elastic across the back of your head. Make sure the elastic is not too tight. Secure the elastic to the other side by tying it through the opposite hole.

Encourage your party guests to wear their fancy sleep masks to bed.

'Note: *Don't use glitter or anything that might get in the sleeper's eyes.*

Beautiful Hair Pieces

Project Difficulty Meter = 1

You and your pals can create gorgeous hair clips together. Trade them with each other, or make them before your party as favors for all your guests.

You'll Need

- ★ metal barrettes
- ★ plain elastic ponytail holders
- ★ fabric headbands
- ★ tiny plastic flowers, ribbons, fur trim
- ★ various fabrics
- ★ assorted sequins or beads
- ★ craft glue

Cover the work surface with newspaper.

Glue the chosen flowers, fabric, sequins, or beads to the barrettes, headbands, and ponytail holders. Let them dry for about an hour. You can simply tie a piece of fur trim or a colored bow to an elastic ponytail holder. Give each guest a small plastic bag or a pretty gift box to hold her beautiful new hair accessories.

While Drying

While you're waiting for your hair pieces to dry, play Ask It Anything in chapter 4.

Quick Scrunchie Update: Take an old scrunchie (that fabric-covered elastic used for holding back hair), and dress it up by tying a pretty ribbon around it.

Cool Caps

Project Difficulty Meter = 2

Create your own super-cool look. Ask your friends to bring a baseball cap or a painter's cap to decorate. If you and your guests are playing the games in chapters 4 through 6, why not choose team colors and pick out team names? Create hats to support the team.

You'll Need

- ★ baseball caps/painters' caps for each guest
- ★ fabric paints
- ★ fabric glue
- ★ an assortment of beads, sequins, and rhinestones

Cover the work surface with newspaper.

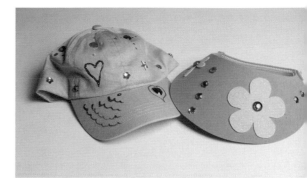

First, decide on a name for each team. Then select team colors and design a team logo with your teammates. Draw the team name and logo onto the hats, and adorn them with beads, sequins, and rhinestones using glue. Allow about an hour for the glue to dry. Wear your caps when you play the games and root for your team. How cool!

Alternate: If you are not playing the games in this book, you can still encourage your guests to create personalized hats that capture each girl's personality.

Decoupage Boxes

Project Difficulty Meter = 2

Make beautiful boxes to keep your treasured items safe. Ask guests to bring a small empty box and a few old magazines. (Crafts stores carry boxes in many sizes and shapes.)

You'll Need

- ★ glossy magazines or strips of colored tissue paper
- ★ scissors
- ★ cardboard boxes of assorted sizes
- ★ lacquer glue

Cover the work surface with newspaper.

With scissors, cut out pictures from your favorite magazines, or use pieces of tissue paper. Glue the paper scraps onto the box. Let dry. Brush on a top layer of lacquer glue over your paper decorations. For a sparkling effect, add glitter to the glue. Let the box dry overnight before touching it.

While Drying

While you're waiting for the glue to dry, make some yummy dessert for later on. How about the chocolate Turtles in chapter 9? (This recipe makes a lot, so your guests can take some home tomorrow.) Or, take a break and enjoy some fresh veggies and dip!

Sweet Sachets

Project Difficulty Meter = 1.5

A sachet is a perfect packet of fragrance. Sachets can be displayed on your dresser in little jars or boxes, or add a fresh scent to your sock drawer. If you attach a ribbon, the sachets can hang from a doorknob.

Make these before the party and give one to each girl as a party favor, or have the guests make them with you. If you plan to make them with your guests, ask them to bring ribbons and fabric pieces from home. You can supply the potpourri and maybe a little scent. Try sweet almond, coconut, lemon, or lavender.

You'll Need

* ★ fabric pieces
* ★ assorted ribbons or colored twine
* ★ scissors
* ★ potpourri
* ★ cotton balls
* ★ light scents

Cover the work surface with newspaper.

Begin with a fabric circle. To make the circle, trace the outline of a dinner plate onto your fabric with a pen and cut along the circle with scissors. For each sachet, add a little potpourri in the fabric circle and fold the fabric over it.

Seal the fabric by cinching it with a ribbon tied around the opening.

Alternate: Instead of potpourri, take three to five cotton balls and pour a few droplets of scent on them. Put the cotton balls in the center of the circle. Fold the fabric over and gather it around the cotton balls and seal the fabric with a ribbon.

Friendship Sleepover Box

Project Difficulty Meter = 3

These friendship boxes are handy for transporting photos, magazines, games, and other mementos to a sleepover.

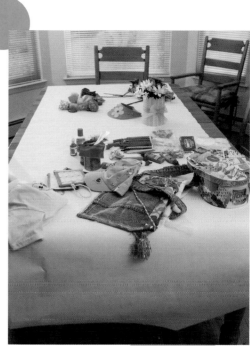

You'll Need

* wrapping paper scraps, magazine scraps, an old calendar
* tape
* heavy carton or shoebox with removable lid
* ribbons
* felt-tip pens
* scissors
* stickers

Cover the work surface with newspaper.

Cover the box with wrapping paper, magazines, or an old calendar; secure with tape. Wrap and tape the box lid separately. Decorate the box with stickers, ribbons, and messages written with a felt-tip pen. Whenever someone in your group has a sleepover, bring the friendship sleep box and fill it with photos and other memories.

9

Food Fest

If the kitchen is your favorite room in the house, grab an apron and get cooking. Your friends can help you prepare these edible delights. Make sure to clean the counters and the dishes as you go, and ask an adult to supervise.

Snacks

★ Veggie plates and fruit platters are healthful and delicious. You can cut up the fruits and veggies beforehand. Arrange the food on pretty platters, and serve with small paper plates and napkins. Add yogurt to make a great dip for the fruit. Buy and serve a ranch or onion dip for the veggies.

★ Popcorn is always fun to eat. You and your guests can experiment with fun toppings. Try grated cheese or drizzle chocolate syrup over the hot popcorn.

★ Make your own trail mix using peanuts, shredded coconut, raisins, pieces of pretzel sticks, and chocolate candies.

★ Concoct a sparkling punch. Mix together seltzer, orange juice, and a container of orange or cherry sherbet. Top with sliced strawberries. Pour this yummy mixture into a punch bowl and keep replenishing it through the evening. Yum!

Make an easy fondue by melting milk chocolate or dark chocolate chips over a low heat or in a double boiler until the mixture is smooth. (Let a parent help. It's easy to burn the chocolate.) Allow to cool for a few minutes. Transfer into a bowl.

What to dip in the fondue
* banana slices
* cherries
* strawberries
* pineapple slices
* chunks of store-bought pound cake
* pretzels
* marshmallows

Dinners

Chicken Nachos

Chicken, cheese, and crunch!

You'll Need
* cooked rotisserie chicken (fresh and hot from the supermarket)
* tortilla chips
* shredded nacho cheese (usually a blend of cheddar, Colby, and Monterey Jack cheeses)
* store-bought salsa (use on the side)

Remove and discard the chicken skin, and cut the white-meat chicken into bite-size pieces. Cover the surface of a baking sheet with aluminum foil (for easy cleanup). Then spread a layer of tortilla chips over the foil. Next arrange some chicken over the chips. Sprinkle cheese over the chicken pieces and chips. Cover all that with more chips. Add more chicken pieces and top the whole thing with cheese.

Bake at 350 degrees F (175 degrees C) for about 10 minutes or until the cheese is melted.

Serve with a bowl of your favorite salsa.

Make Your Own Pizza

Sure, you can order from the local pizza parlor, but this is a delicious and cheap alternative!

You'll Need

★ several loaves of fresh Italian bread, sliced
★ canned tomato or pizza sauce
★ grated mozzarella and Parmesan cheese

Various toppings

★ pepperoni slices
★ cooked spinach
★ chopped broccoli
★ cooked hamburger
★ mushrooms
★ pepper slices
★ black olives, sliced
★ diced ham

Give everyone a large slice of Italian bread. Have guests spoon on tomato or pizza sauce onto the bread and then add cheese and whatever toppings they like.

Bake on a cookie sheet at 350 degrees F (175 degrees C) for 10 minutes or until the cheese melts and begins to brown.

Taco Pies

Hearty and easy but spicy. You'll need an adult helper.

You'll Need

★ 2 packages of Pillsbury Crescent refrigerated dough

Taco Filling

★ 1 pound of lean ground beef
★ small diced onion
★ ½ teaspoon cumin powder
★ 1 teaspoon chili powder
★ 2 Tablespoons chopped cilantro
★ minced clove of garlic
★ 8-ounce (225-g) can of tomato paste
★ cooking oil

★ grated cheese (mozzarella or taco cheeses)

In a pan, heat up a few Tablespoons of oil and sauté the onion and garlic. Add the meat and the rest of the seasonings. Cook until the meat is no longer pink. Add the tomato paste. Stir. Bring to a simmer.

Cover the base and sides of a 9-inch (about 22.5-cm) pie plate with triangles from the two packages of uncooked crescent dough. Spoon the cooked meat over the dough. Then cover that with a blanket of cheese.

Bake at 375 degrees F (190 degrees C) for about 15 minutes, or until the cheese is melted and the crust is golden.

Build-a-Salad

Salad makes a light and healthful meal.

You'll Need
* romaine lettuce torn into bite-size pieces
* diced celery
* shredded carrots
* sliced cucumbers
* cherry tomatoes
* chopped cauliflower
* sliced peppers
* assortment of salad dressings

Add Any of These
* grated cheese
* sliced hard-boiled eggs
* chunks of cold chicken
* tuna chunks
* croutons
* sunflower seeds

Arrange each ingredient in a separate bowl with a serving spoon. Have each guest build a salad and then add the desired extras.

Desserts

S'mores

A favorite among Brownies and Girl Scouts, this yummy treat can be made in different ways. Here's a no-brainer recipe that tastes out of this world.

You'll Need

* ★ box of graham crackers
* ★ bunch of chocolate bars
* ★ bag of marshmallows

Break a graham cracker in half. On one half, place a square or two of chocolate, and top that with a marshmallow. Cover with the second graham cracker half, and cook in the microwave for about 20 seconds (the marshmallow should puff out, but not explode). Eat.

Fruity Fun

Fruit lovers unite! This is a kind of fruit compote. Ask an adult to help.

You'll Need

* ★ 12 pieces of fruit—mostly peaches, plums, strawberries, and cherries
* ★ water
* ★ ½ cup of sugar
* ★ whipped cream

Place all the fruits and the water in a large saucepan on a low heat. Let simmer for about an hour. Then pour in the sugar.

Let the fruit mixture cool.

Pour the fruit mixture into a blender and puree until it is smooth.

Spoon the fruit compote into pretty bowls and top with whipped cream.

Turtles

These turtles are yummy chocolate and butterscotch treats. Let your guests take home the leftovers as party favors. You'll need an adult helper.

You'll Need

★ 2 cups (480 ml) semisweet chocolate chips
★ 2 cups (480 ml) butterscotch chips
★ 1½-ounce (42-g) can of salted cocktail peanuts
★ 5 ounces (140 g) chow mein noodles

Melt the chocolate and butterscotch chips together slowly in a saucepan on a low heat. When the chocolate and the butterscotch have melted, add the nuts and noodles.

Drop by heaping teaspoons onto a cookie sheet lined with waxed paper. Let cool.

Store in the fridge in an airtight container. This should make about five dozen cookies.

Breakfast

Wake up, sleepy heads!

Berry Crepes

Life is berry good! Don't worry; even if your crepe comes out a little sloppy, it will still be delicious. You'll need an adult helper.

You'll Need

- ★ eggs
- ★ low-fat milk
- ★ cooking oil spray
- ★ sliced strawberries, raspberries, and blueberries
- ★ powdered sugar

Beat an egg and $\frac{1}{2}$ cup (120 ml) of low-fat milk together. Whisk in another $\frac{1}{8}$ cup (30 ml) of milk if you want to make the batter thin.

Spray a skillet with cooking oil spray and put on the burner on medium heat. Pour the batter into the frying pan in a large circle. Toss blueberries, strawberries, and raspberries over the mixture. Cook until small bubbles form. Then, flip and cook the other side for a few minutes.

With a big spatula, lift the finished crepe (a thin, delicate pancake) onto a plate. Roll it up, sprinkle with powdered sugar, and add more berries on top.

This recipe makes enough for two crepes.

Strawberries-and-Cream Biscuits

This dreamy dessert doubles for breakfast! If you like things sweet, add a little sugar to the whipped cream.

You'll Need

- ★ ready-made biscuits (or the heat-and-serve kind)
- ★ sliced strawberries
- ★ fresh whipped cream

Pile strawberries and whipped cream in between two room-temperature biscuits.

Each serving requires two biscuits, $\frac{1}{2}$ cup of sliced strawberries, and 2 Tablespoons of whipped cream. Yum.

10

Goodie Bags and Good-bye Gifts

Give your guests something to remember the great time they had at your party. They'll love you for it. Feel free to give these gifts before, during, or after the party.

Fruity Lip Gloss

You didn't know you could make your own cosmetics, did you? Make this *scent-sational* lip gloss and wrap it in colored cellophane and ribbons. Label it with a sticker.

For each lip gloss, you need

★ 2 Tablespoons (30 ml) solid shortening
★ 1 Tablespoon (15 ml) fruit-flavored powdered-drink mix
★ 35-mm film container or small container, empty and thoroughly washed

Combine the shortening and the powdered-drink mix in a microwave-safe bowl.

Place in the microwave on high for about 30 seconds or until it becomes a liquid. Pour the mixture into the containers. Place into the fridge for at least a half hour, while the mixture hardens.

Ideally, you'd want to sterilize the small containers. Ask your mom for ideas.

Vanilla Scrub

Here's a sweet treat, not to eat, but to use for scrubbing in the shower. Your skin is left feeling smooth as silk and smelling heavenly. It's for all skin types.

For each person, you'll need
- ½ cup (120 ml) kosher salt
- ½ cup (120 ml) baby oil
- 1 Tablespoon (15 ml) vanilla extract
- small decorative jar
- pretty bow or sticker

Mix the ingredients together and pour into individual jars. It's a delightful scrub to use in the shower.

Wash and Go

Wrap a colorful washcloth and a toothbrush in a pretty little shopping bag with colored tissue paper, and you've got a great goodie bag to give as the party gets underway. It's also useful, especially if one of your guests forgot something from home!

Sock It to Me

A pair of ankle socks and a few hard candies tossed into a colored cellophane bag says thanks for coming to my party.

Nail Time

Make individual nail kits for each guest. For each, you'll need a nail file, an emery board, some cotton balls, and nail polish. Put the stuff in a small plastic bag or colored cellophane.

Glitz and Go

A purse-size container or two of body glitter or hand cream is a neat thing to give your pals.

Candy to Go

Wrap several chocolate-butterscotch turtles (see page 86) in a small box or in a plastic bag with a ribbon tied around it. Write the person's name on a sticker, and adhere it to the box or the plastic bag.

Hair Me Out!

How about a bunch of scrunchies, headbands, and hair clips wrapped in colored tissue paper and ribbon?

No Party's a Flop

Give everyone a pair of flip-flops with a bow around them. Attach a tag to a flip-flop with the girl's name on it.

Take It Personally

Make or buy note cards that have each guest's first initial on them. Include a pen and some stickers, and you've got a great gift.

Scratch That

Little back-scratchers and a trial-size bottle of lotion make a fun gift.

Photo Op

How about mini photo albums for the photos you took? This is a nice way to say thanks for the laughs and the smiles.

Brush 'n' Go

How about a travel toothbrush and a small container of toothpaste wrapped in a teeny shopping bag? Sweet.

Armed and Fab

A few colored wide rubber-band bracelets look good on anyone's wrist.

★ ★ ★

The laughs. The stories. The secrets. The games. The dancing. The snacks. The things you made. The memories.

Aren't sleepovers awesome? Isn't it time to start planning your next one?

Acknowledgments

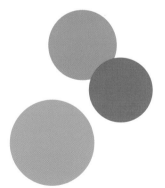

We'd especially like to thank Bob and Cathy Steimle and their children, Natalie and Kevin. We are also grateful to Karen Hopkins and Leighann Martone. Some pajamas were provided by American Marketing Enterprises. We thank Cindy Boudreau, soft-goods engineer, for remaking selected crafts.

Many thanks to parents for lending their time and our models: Natalie Steimle, Bailey McGillian, Devan McGillian, Lauren Egodigwe, Alexa Lodenquai, Gabriella Rocco, Niki Sabot, Hazziza, Sheila, Stephanie, Elizabeth, Johanna, Jackie, Ryanne, Leighann, Emily, Hayley, and a second Lauren.

Index

About the Author

Jamie Kyle McGillian is a reporter for The Rivertowns Enterprise and a substitute teacher. She is the author of *Sidewalk Chalk: Outdoor Fun and Games* (Sterling), *The Kids' Money Book* (Sterling), *The Busy Mom's Book of Preschool Activities* (Sterling), and *On the Job with a Firefighter* (Barron's Juvenile). Ms. McGillian lives with her husband and two daughters, and her pug named Lola along the Hudson River. Her home is the site for many sleepover parties!

Good Night!